Harmonica for Advanced

Harmonica Around the World

2

harmonicabreeze.com

- 3 Octaves Playing
- Riffs, scales
- Classic and folk
- Single notes and chords
- Songs from around the world
- Web Site to practice

Ami Luz

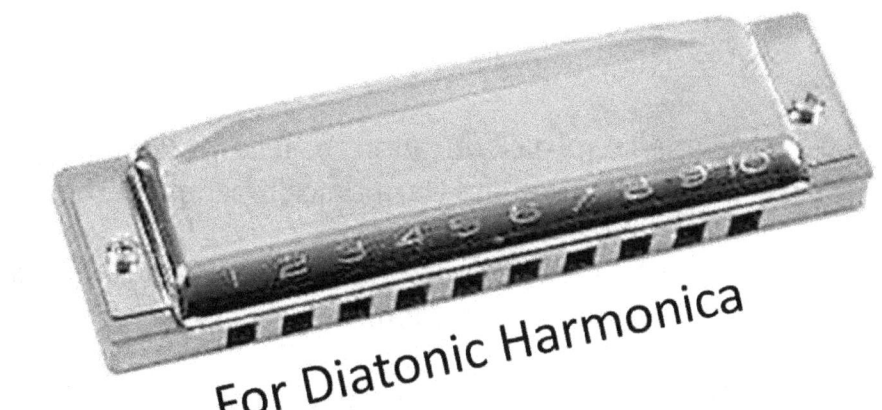

For Diatonic Harmonica

www.harmonicabreeze.com

Musical Breeze Publication *2016* ©

Introduction

About this Book

Harmonica for beginners (Book 2) is a book written for diatonic (blues) harmonica players from around the world that finish "harmonica for Beginners (Book 1) and has the basic skills of playing the harmonica and reading notes.

Advanced students will find many songs and melodies from around the globe to play at the range off three octaves.

The lessons include notes, harmonica playing techniques and chords for guitar accompaniment. Some songs have tabs for the harmonica. Over 50 harmonica songs and exercises for diatonic harmonica plyers.

Ami Luz

Music teacher and musician.

Over 30 years of teaching experience.

Has an M.Ed. degree in music education from Lewinsky College in Israel. Guitar teacher for more than 30 years and Harmonica teacher for the past 12 years.

Ami has written six instructional books for learning various musical instruments, including the ukulele, guitar and harmonica.

There is a new harmonica site that follows the book where you can see and hear Ami playing, play along to a video accompaniment online as well get a support and help thru the site using **contact us** and **Facebook**.

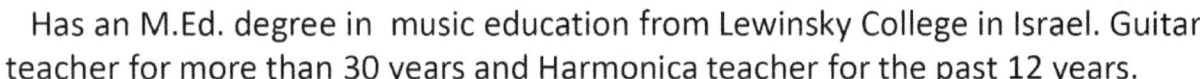

www.harmonicabreeze.com

Contents

Introduction	2
Contents	3
About the Author	4
Diatonic Harmonica – C	5
C Scale - do major	6
One Octave Exercises	7
The note D	9
American songs	10
The note E	11
Six-eight time	12
The note F	13
The note G	14
When Swallows Homeward Fly	15
Mexican Dance	16
The Irish Washerwomen	17
The note A	18
Songs	19
Songs Around the World	20
Songs	21
Famous Challenging Pieces	22
Skater`s Waltz	23
Turkey In The Straw	24
The Sailor's Hornpipe	25
Free music staves for you	27
A Basic Musical Vocabulary	31
The site www.harmonicabreeze.com	32

Introduction

How to learn harmonica

This book has all the instructions you need Progress and improve your playing technique. Learn scales and special playing technics up to 3 octave playing.

The right way to learn and advance properly is by **practicing about 20 minutes every day** .

Don't rush! Read carefully all the instructions and advance step by step.

The best sign that it is time to move on to the next page is when you can play the songs fluently and enjoy your playing.

You've mastered a piece when you can play by ear.

Remember! It's fun to play the harmonica but you have to practice to make music.

Good luck!

www.harmonicabreeze.com

Diatonic Harmonica - C

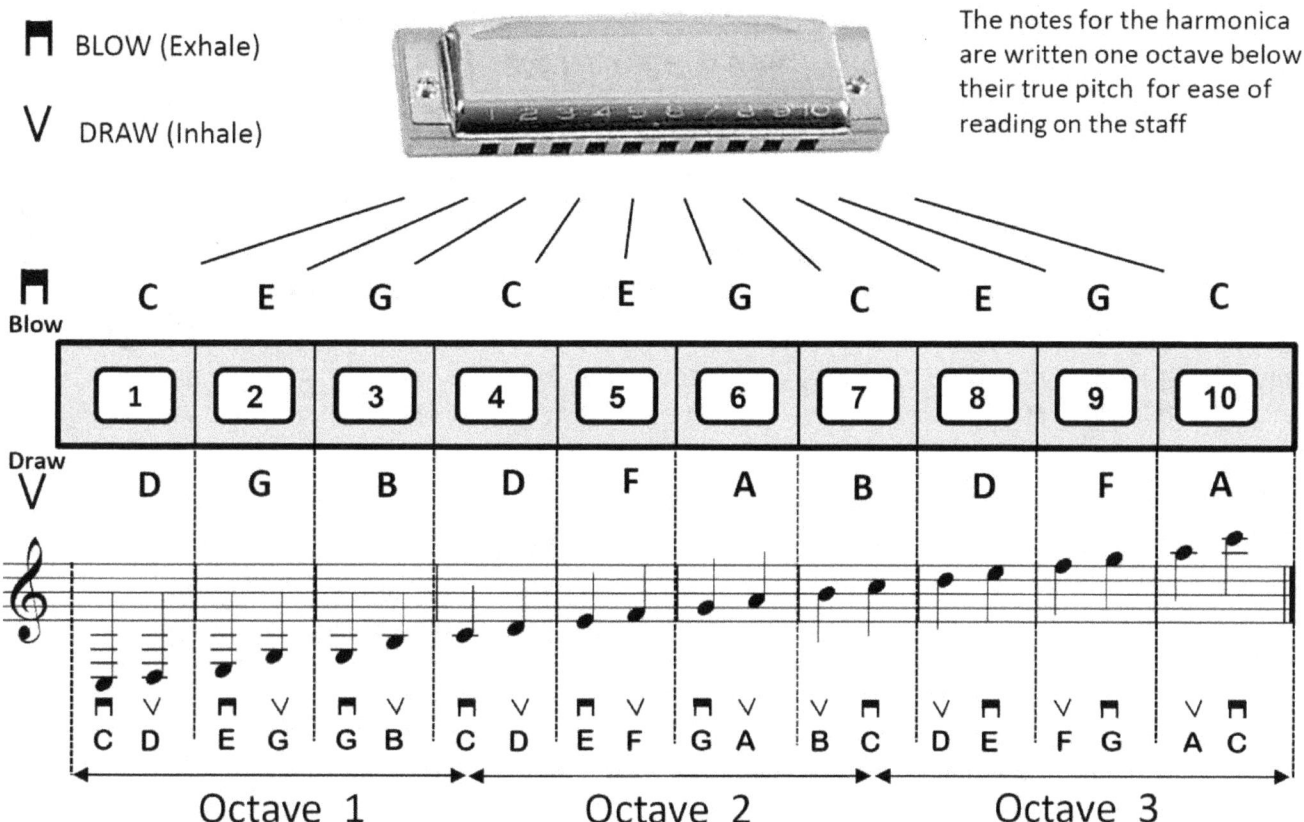

Please note !
There is no F (**fa**) and A (**la**) tones/notes on the first octave, and B (**ti**) note on the third octave. You can reach these note by note bending technique.

Some Diatonic Harmonica Scales

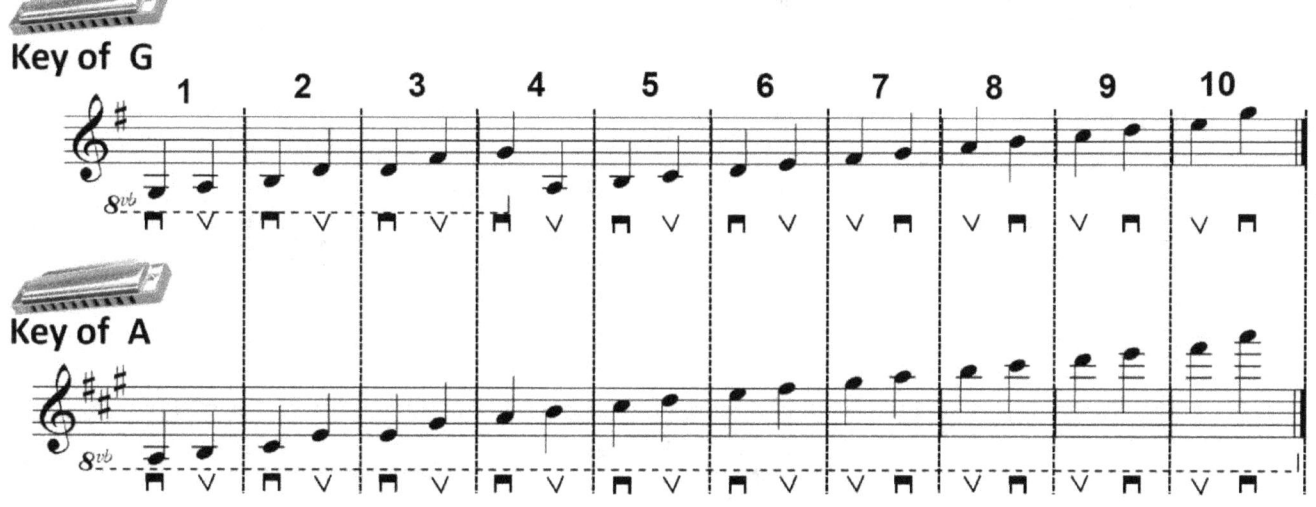

HarmonicaBreeze - Learn To Play Harmonica

C Scale - do major

Now you can play all the notes in the **C major scale**, therefore many songs in one octave.

1 **C Major Scale**

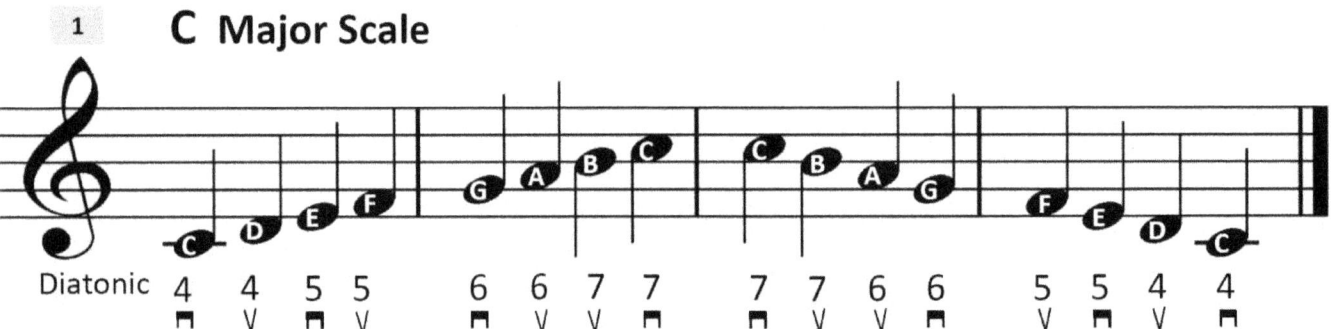

Music Scale
Ascending or descending sequence of tones that are used as building blocks to create melodies and musical compositions.

C Major Scale
Scale which starts with sound **c** (do) and climbs 8 notes to high **c** . On the piano keyboard playing on the white keys only.

One Octave
The interval between two notes that has the same name but difference of eight steps. For example **C1** to **C2**

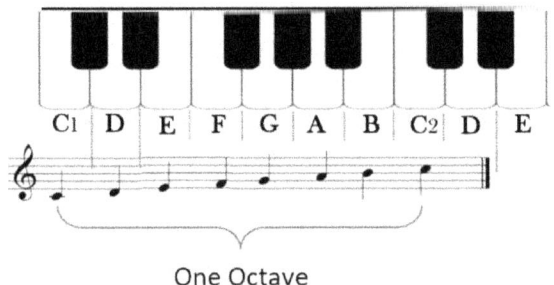

One Octave

2 **Skipping Up**   First play it without Legato.

3 **Skipping Down**

4 **The Scale in Threes**

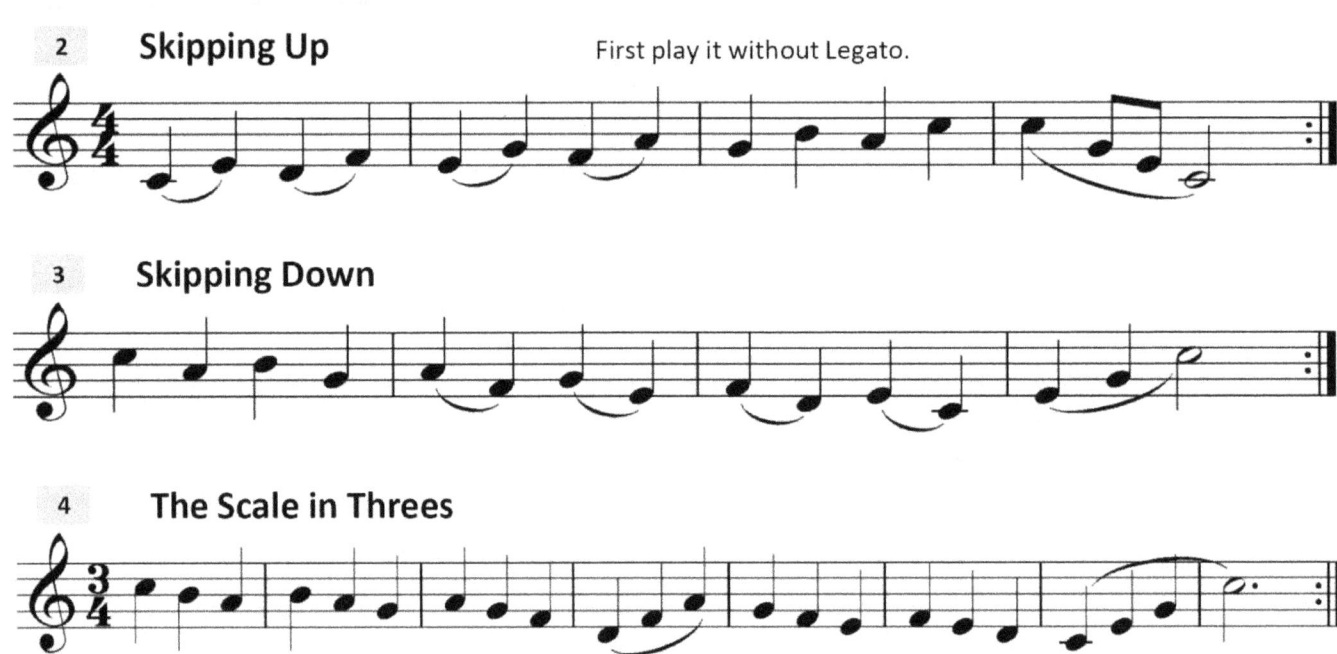

HarmonicaBreeze - Learn To Play Harmonica

One Octave Exercises

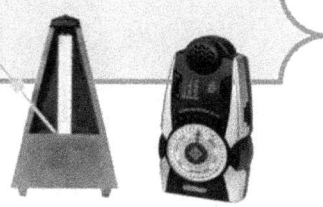
Metronome

These exercises have different rhythms. Play them many times thoroughly. I recommend using a metronome to keep time accurately. A **Metronome** is a mechanical or electronic device that plays the beat or pulse according to the number of beats per minute. You can set it to play the beat you feel most comfortable at.

5 **Along the C Scale**

6 **Jumps and Intervals**

Moderato

7 **Syncopated Rhythm**

Allegro

8 **Irish Style**

Allegro

9 **In the Dorian Mode**

Adagio

Dorian Mode - An Ancient Greek Scale

HarmonicaBreeze - Learn To Play Harmonica

10 In the A Minor Scale
Moderato

11 Triplets

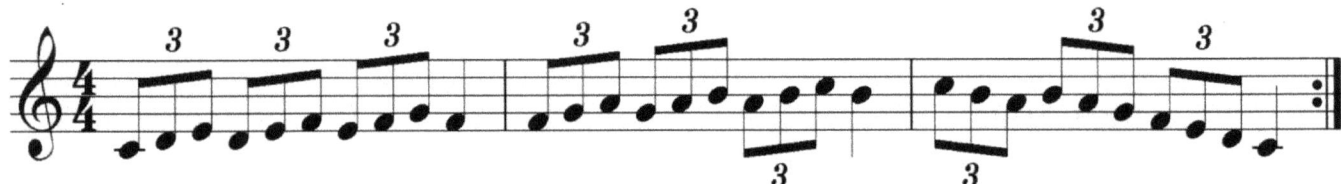

12 Play the Swing
Moderato

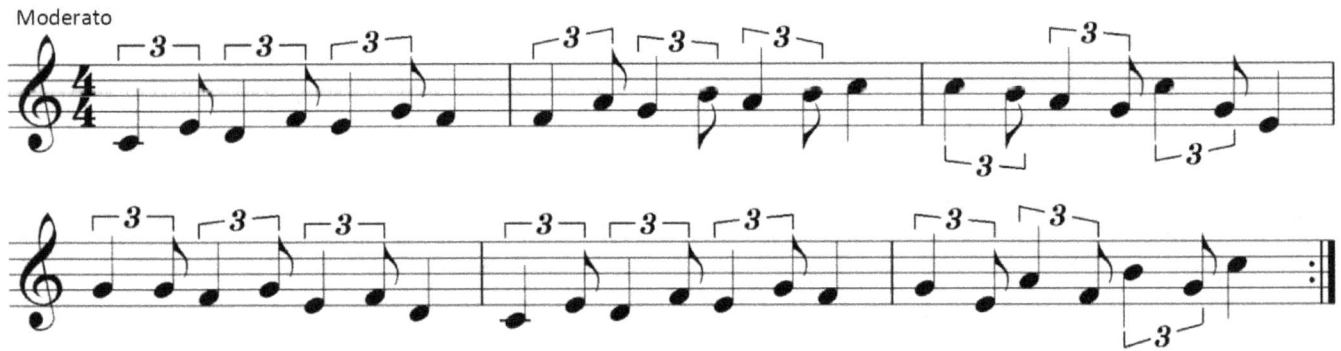

13 Play faster

14 Play legato

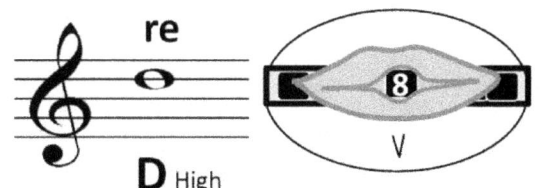

The note D

Diatonic Hole   8 ⌄ (Draw)

15 The Beetle

Cross Harp

When we're playing a different scale from the harmonica scale. For example: we are playing a C harmonica and **Scarborough Fair** is written in the Dorian mode so we are playing **cross harp**

Dorian Scale

Antique Greek scale. Starting with the note **D** and climbing up to **D2**. The song **Scarborough Fair** is written in the **D Dorian mode**

16 Scarborough Fair

English song

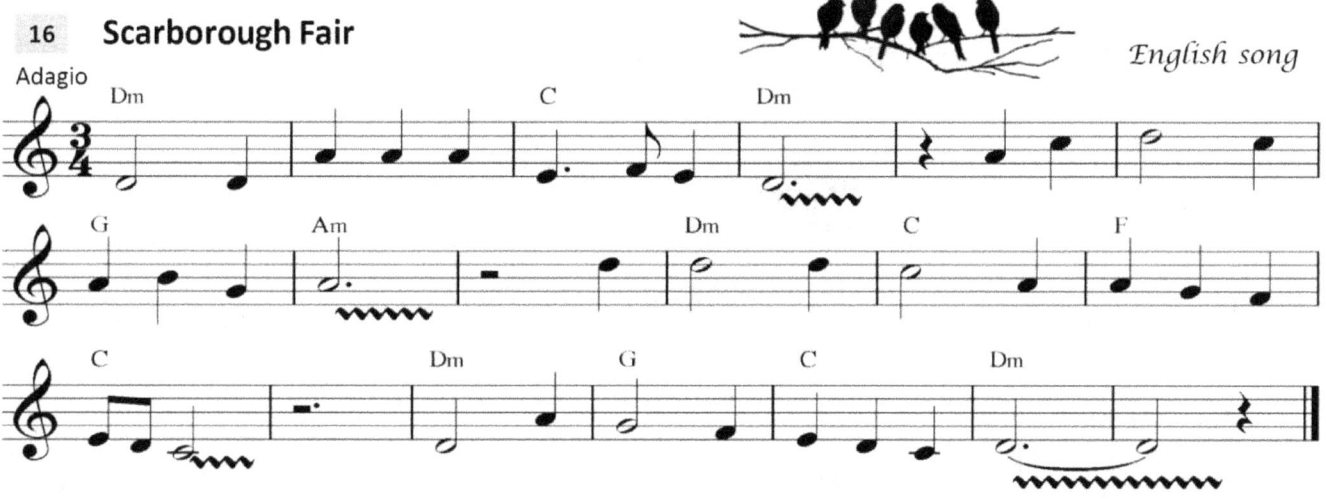

Note: The song "Drunken Sailor" leaps down a whole octave on bars 10 and 12 so you should practice these bars separately in order to perform a clean, accurate and fast leaps.

17 Drunken Sailor

American song

HarmonicaBreeze - Learn To Play Harmonica

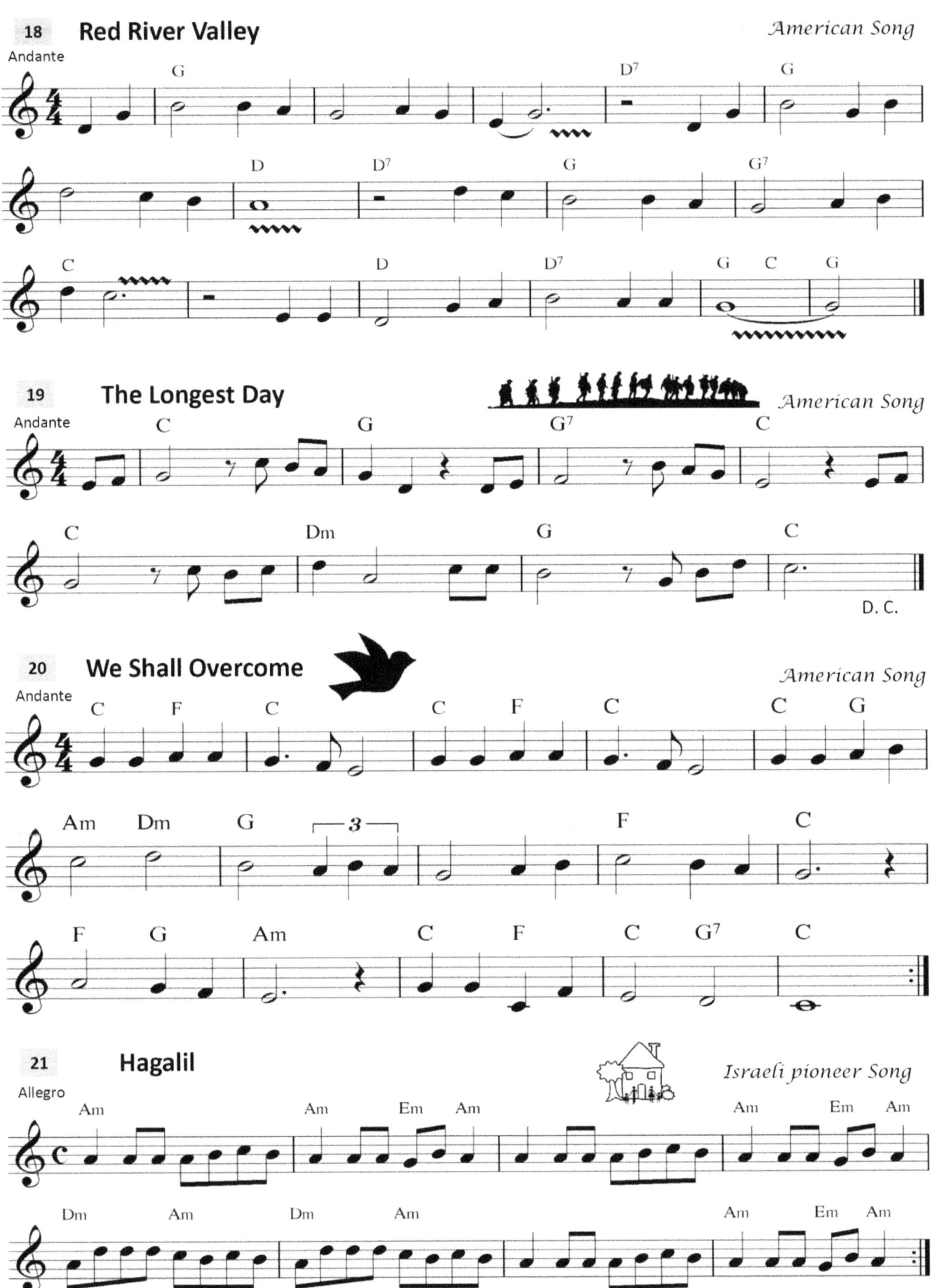

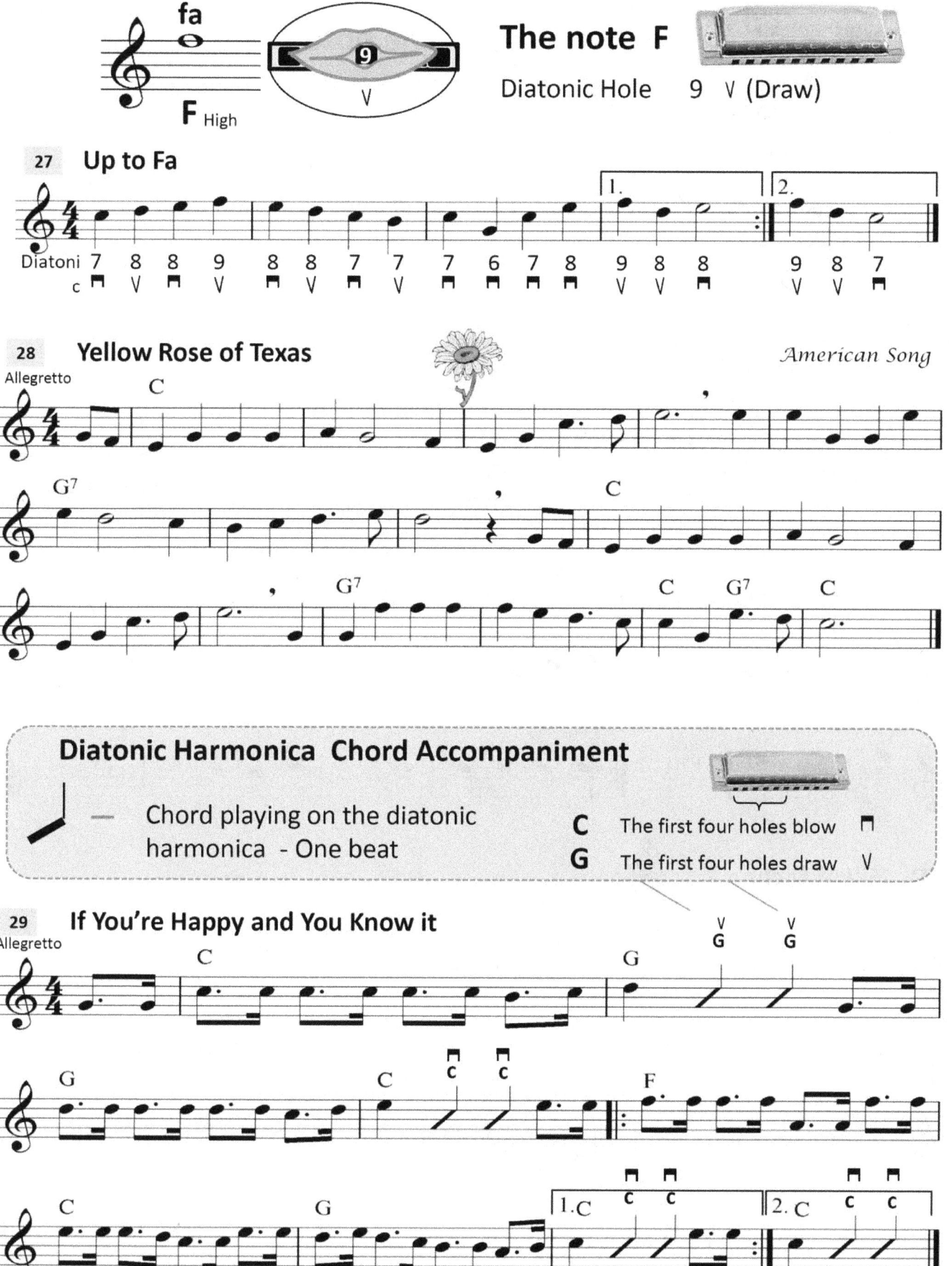

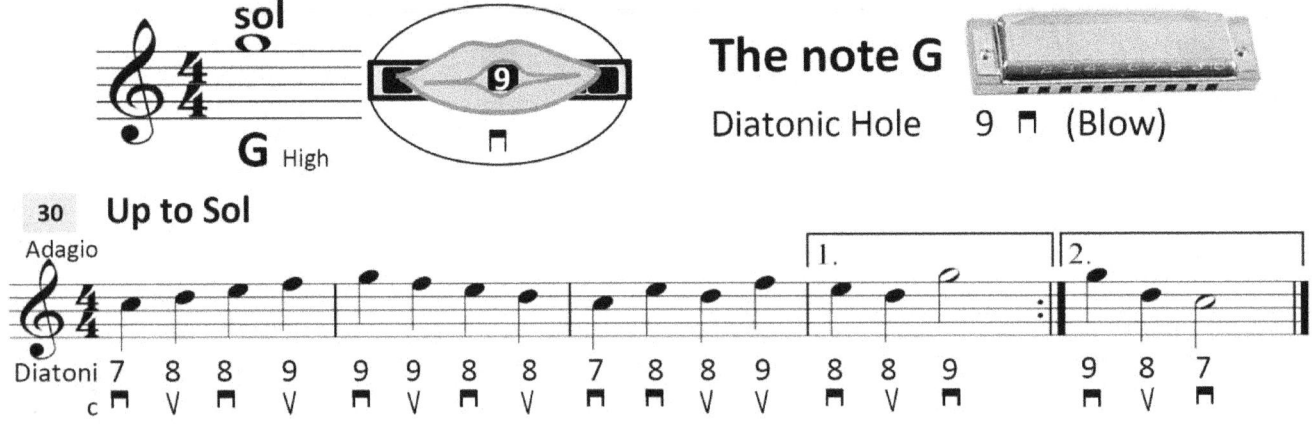

The note G

Diatonic Hole   9 ⊓ (Blow)

30   **Up to Sol**

Adagio

Diatonic: 7 8 8 9 9 9 8 8 7 8 8 9 | 8 8 9 | 9 8 7

Note: You can now go back and play the tunes you played at the beginning of this book, but an octave higher. This is good practice!

Alla Breve

Time Signature counting two beats to a bar.
Each half note gets one beat.

31   **Spring has Come Again**

Babylon

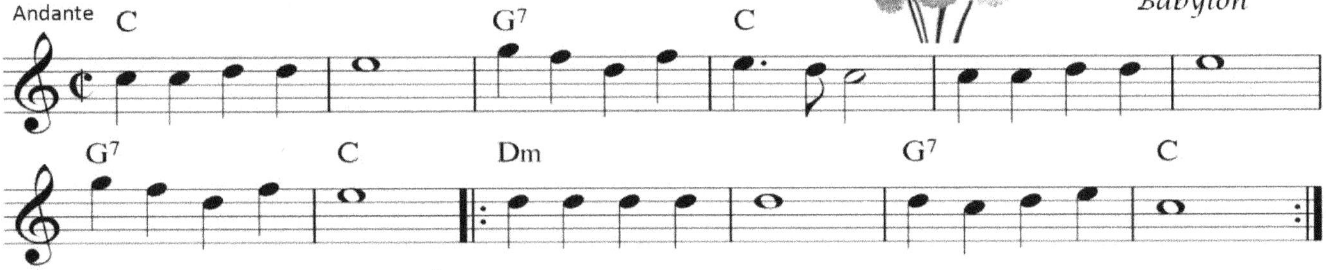

Andante

32   **Silent Night**

Christmas carol

Adagio

Rit.

HarmonicaBreeze - Learn To Play Harmonica

Note:
Once you learn to play this beautiful song, try to play it an octave lower on the chromatic harmonica.

Duet for two diatonic harmonica players

Diatonic 4 Holes blow | Diatonic 4 Holes draw | Do not play. Rest 1 beat

Instructions:

This cheerful song should start slowly and accelerate (get faster).
You can accompany the song on the diatonic harmonica with short quick puffs – chords - as marked in the score.

36 The Irish Washerwomen   *Irish Song*

Allegro

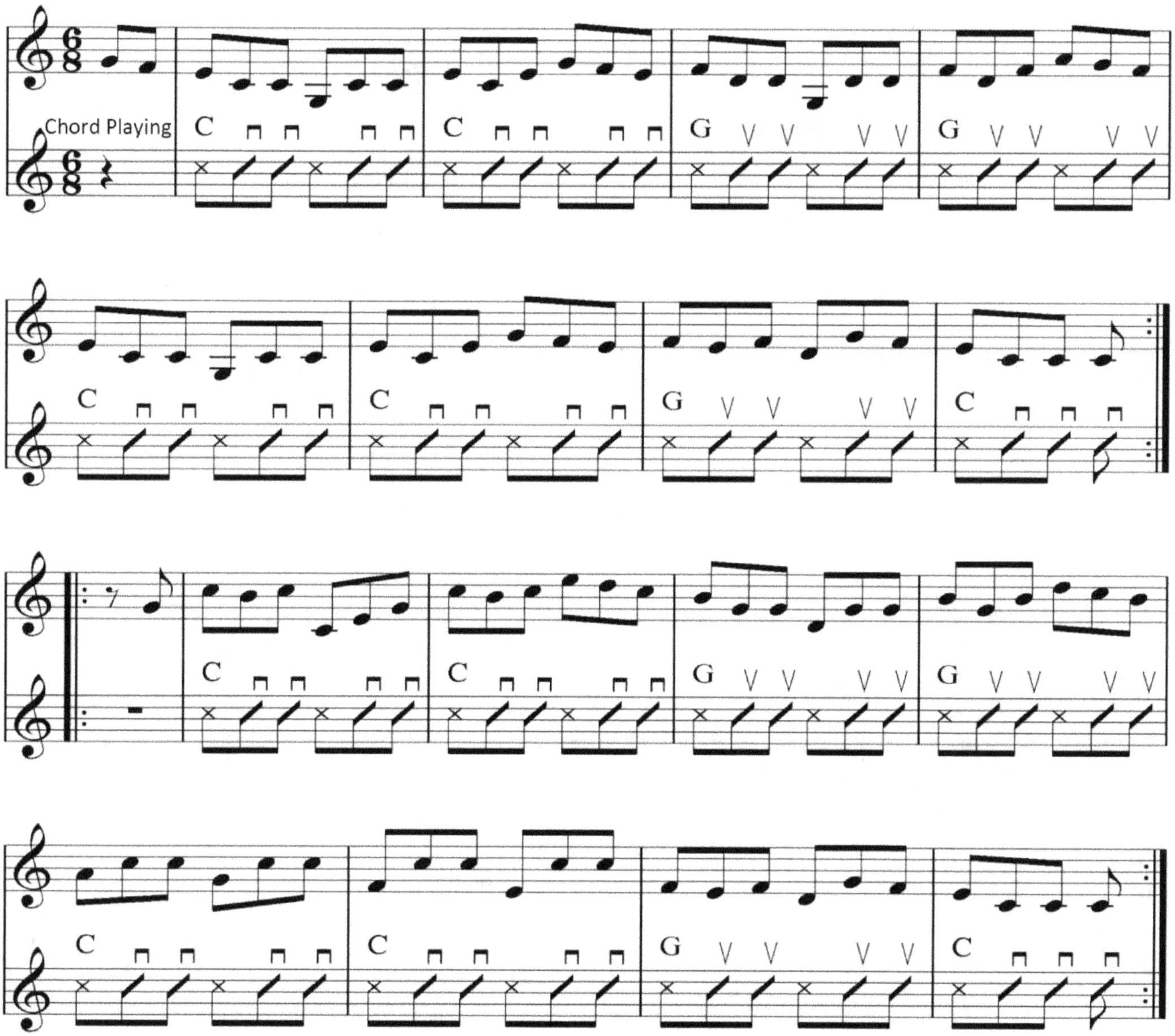

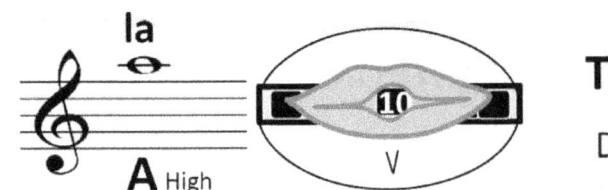
The Note A
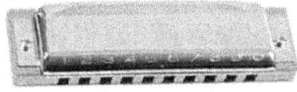

Diatonic Hole   10   V (Draw)

Note:
As you ascend the scale, you should blow stronger and concentrate on your tone.

37 Slowly To the Top

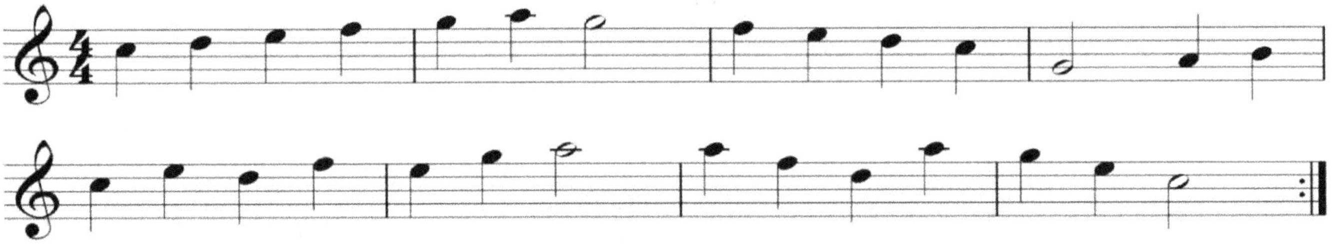

38 Danny Boy (Londonderry Air)   *Irish Song*

Slowly and with feeling

Songs Around the World

42 Heimatland (Pentatonic scale)  *Thailand song*

43 Um die Muhle *Slowakei song*
Moderato

44 Lambada *Bolivian song*
Allegretto

Famous Challenging Pieces

Note:
Here is a country song, cheerful and quick. Playing legato allows you to play faster. Pay attention to the staccato notes.

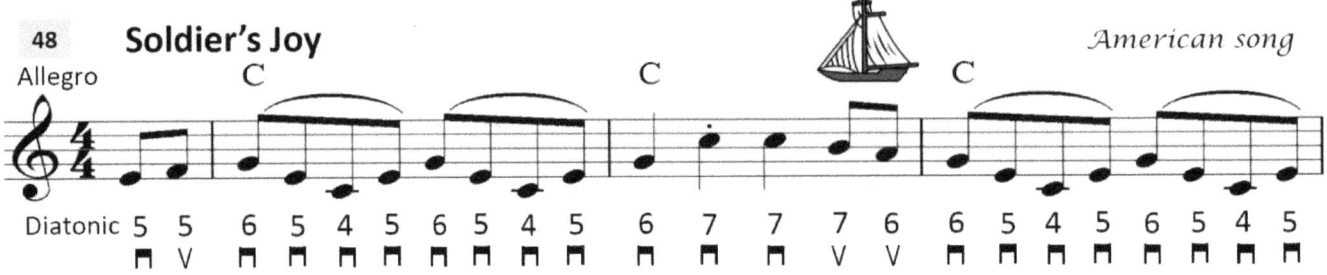

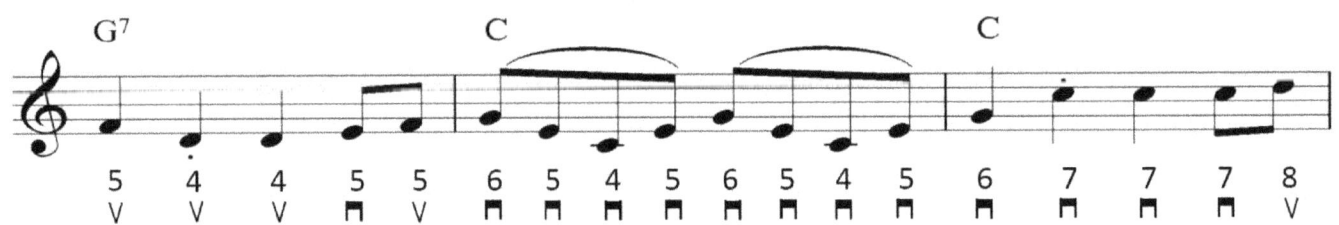

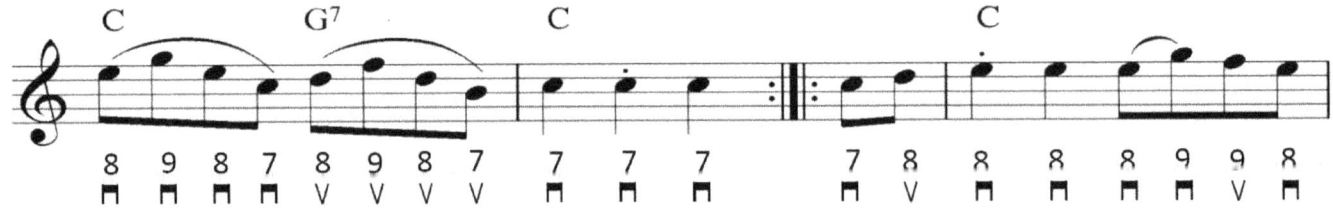

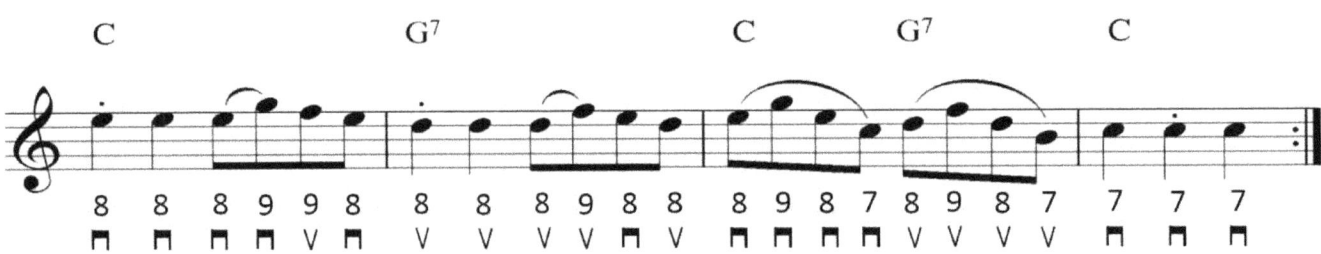

Note! Please note the legato and staccato markings in this happy country tune.
In the fourth line, play the low notes the first time and high notes on second time, as written.
It is recommended to play the song on the A or G scale harmonica which lower and a bit more mellow.
We recommend playing with a guitar accompaniment, or using a metronome.

50 Turkey In The Straw

English country song

Note! This cheerful melody uses two bends, **G sharp** - played like **A Flat** hole **6 half step bend**, and **B to A** hole **3** - **two steps bend**

You can add legato where you feel it is appropriate. When playing the final section, bars 28 to 30, you should change to a D Harmonica (as indicated) unless you are using a Chromatic Harmonica.

51 The Sailor's Hornpipe

English sailor's dance

 # Free music staves for you

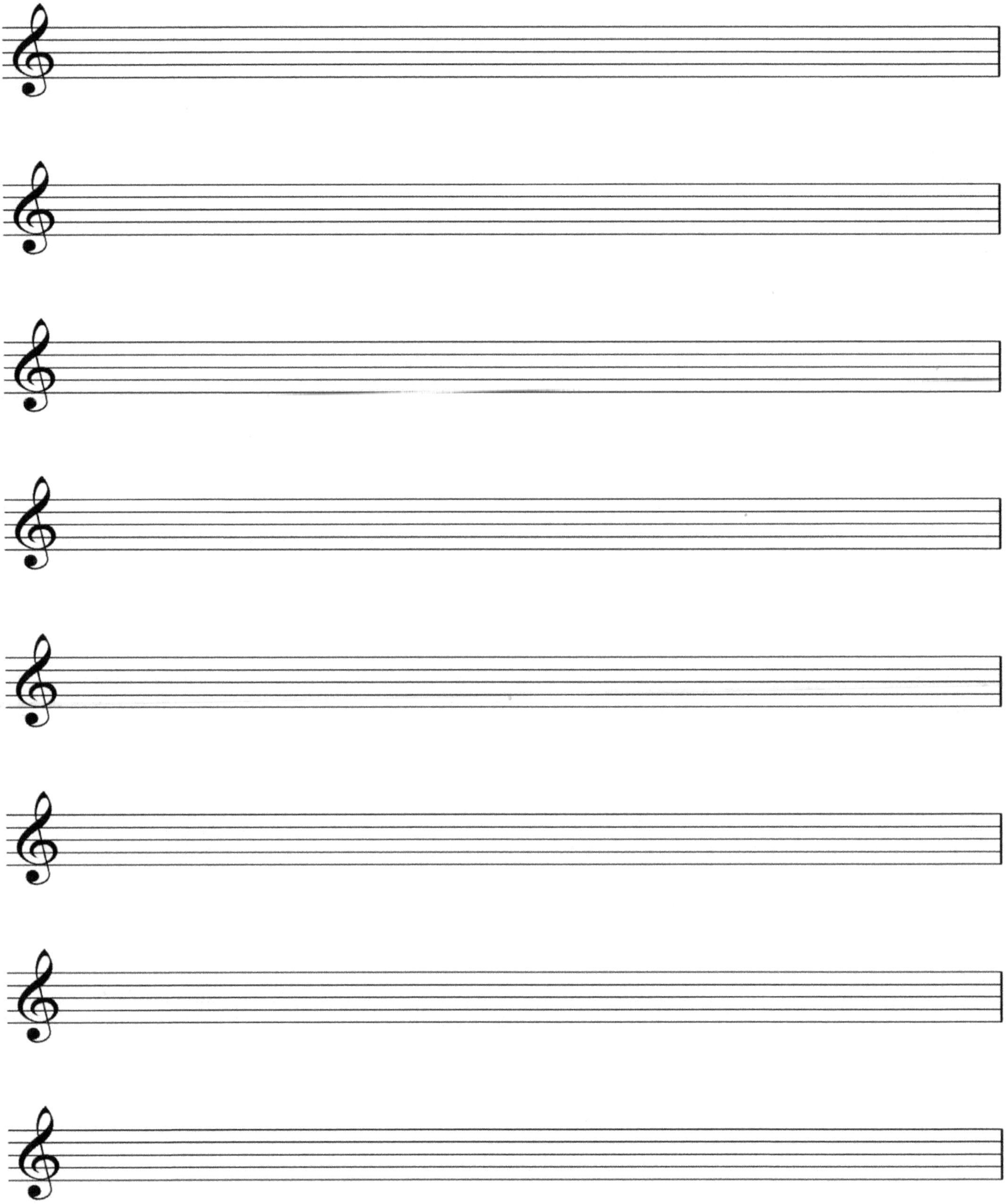

Basic Musical Vocabulary

Dynamics - relative volume level in music

PP - pianissimo - very soft/quiet
P - piano - soft / quiet
mp - mezzo piano - somewhat soft
mf - mezzo forte - somewhat loud
f - forte - loud / strong
ff - fortissimo - very loud

Cres.   Crescendo
getting louder

dim.   Diminuendo
getting softer

Tempo - the speed of the music (BPM- beat per minute)

adagio - slow - 66 – 76 (BPM)
andante - walking speed - 76 – 108 (BPM)
moderato - medium speed - 108 – 120 (BPM)
allegro - fast - 120 – 168 (BPM)
presto - very fast - 168 – 200 (BPM)

acc. accelerando
getting faster

rit. ritardando
getting slower

C major scale - two octaves

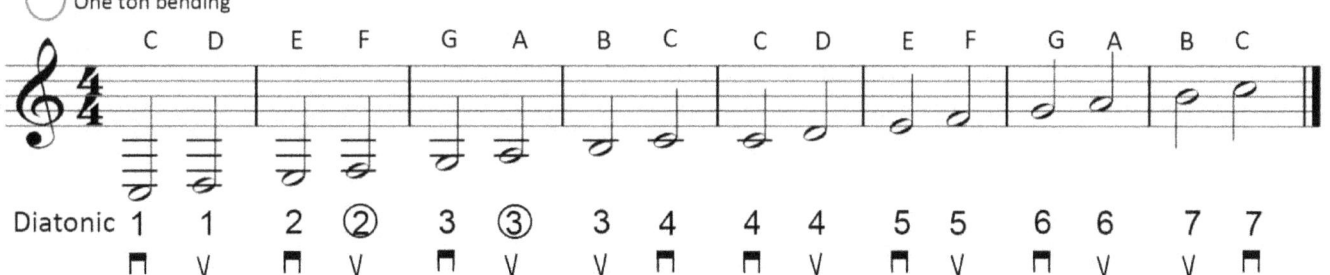

A minor scale - two octaves

www.harmonicabreeze.com

Harmonicabreeze.com
Site accompanies this book

 Each lesson contains video clips

 Get teacher help thru mail or face book

 Free lessons to try

When you hold a Harmonica,
a whole world of music is in your hands
Use it anywhere you can

Ami Luz

Good Luck!

www.ingramcontent.com/pod-product-compliance
Lightning Source LLC
Chambersburg PA
CBHW081503040426
42446CB00016B/3377